The Wonder Series

Bats

Swift Shadows in the Twilight

Written
by
Ann C. Cooper

Illustrated
by
Gail Kohler Opsahl
and
Marjorie C. Leggitt

Denver Museum of Natural History
and Roberts Rinehart Publishers

Thank You

Dr. Merlin Tuttle, Executive Director of Bat Conservation International, for sharing your knowledge, enthusiasm, and fascinating bat anecdotes, and for reviewing *Bats: Swift Shadows in the Twilight.*

Dr. Rick Adams, Colorado Bat Society, for teaching me to recognize the clicking of pallid bats, and for reviewing this book.

Steven J. Bissell, Head of Environmental Education, Colorado Division of Wildlife; Dr. Mark Bogen, U.S. Fish and Wildlife Service; Dr. Stephen P. Cross, Southern Oregon State College; Nan Hall and Earl Matsui, Woodland Park Zoo, Seattle; the staff of the High Desert Museum in Bend, Oregon, for patiently answering my many questions about bats and what it is like to work with them.

And thanks to my husband, who cheerfully accompanied me on many bat-quests, and who let me bounce as many ideas off him as a bat bounces echoes off its prey!

—*Ann C. Cooper*

Published in the United States of America by Roberts Rinehart Publishers, Post Office Box 666, Niwot, Colorado 80544

Published in Great Britain, Ireland, and Europe by Roberts Rinehart Publishers, Main Street, Schull, West Cork, Republic of Ireland

Distributed in the United States and Canada by Publishers Group West

Library of Congress Catalog Card Number 93-85479

International Standard Book Number 1-879373-52-1

Manufactured in the United States of America

Contents

Introducing Bats

*Y*ou may see them as swift shapes scrawling sky trails across a woodland clearing at dusk. You may glimpse fast-beating wings flitting above a pond as night falls. You may see shadowy outlines flying above a park in the twilight . . .

Even if you have never seen one bat before, you will probably recognize the shadowy shapes as bats. Bats are familiar to nearly everyone—from Halloween images and stories, if not from real life. Yet most people have never seen a bat up close.

Bats seek food at night. They move quickly. They avoid people. They sleep by day. Many seek dark shelters such as caves, mines, or hollow trees. Others sleep in the open. They blend so well with their surroundings, you could walk right by and never even notice them. For these reasons, bats are not easy to find or study. Even if you are out and about at bat-time, you will have only fleeting views of bats—not long, good looks at them. You will have difficulty proving or disproving your ideas about bats just by watching them.

No wonder that when it comes to bats, many people are not sure where fact ends and fantasy begins.

Are bats dirty and dangerous? Do bats get tangled in your hair? Are vampire bats enormous? Do they suck pints of blood? The answer to all of these questions is no! Later in this book you will find the true details.

Many folktales from around the world offer fanciful ideas about bats. Stories were a way people in the past tried to explain the animals around them. Did Bat get his wings from drum leather? Does Bat have short legs because she fell from a cliff? Does Bat fly at night because he is trying to put tatters of darkness back in his basket? You can find answers to these and other bat questions in the stories in this book.

You may half-believe supernatural stories that link bats with the evil forces of darkness, witches, spooks, or Halloween. You may wonder about Count Dracula in his dark, flowing cloak that looks like wings. All these stories are pure fantasy—just spooky fun. They have nothing to do with real bats.

Fact, folktale, and fantasy are all a part of people's ideas about bats. Later in this book you will see that the truth about bats is more astonishing than any of the stories about them.

5

The Bat and the Weasels

Once, a bat slipped from his roost in a tree and fell to the ground. A hungry weasel was hunting beneath the tree. A good meal, he thought, as he snapped at the bat.

"Help me! Mercy! Save me!" the bat cried, knowing he was about to die.

"Why should I save you?" asked the weasel. "You are my enemy. In fact you are my worst enemy among the birds."

"But I am not a bird," said the bat. "See my fur? See my teeth? I'm a sort of flying mouse."

"Then I suppose I'll let you go," the weasel said.

Later, the same bat slipped from his roost again. He was caught by a different weasel, who happened to be hunting beneath the tree.

"I shall eat you," said the weasel. "I fancy a tasty mouse for dinner."

"But I am not a mouse," said the bat. "Look at my wings."

"Then I suppose you are a bird. I will let you go," the second weasel said.

And so twice the bat went free.

The moral of this fable is to be flexible in the face of danger!

Retold from a fable by Aesop, a legendary storyteller of Ancient Greece

6

Bat Basics

Many folktales hint that people were not always sure how bats fit into the animal kingdom. They saw that bats had four legs and fur, and looked a bit like mice. They also knew bats flew through the air like birds. Are bats mice? Are they birds? Are they something else? What is the truth?

Bats are mammals.

© Bats have fur. Even though "Halloween" bats are always shown as pure black, many real bats have colorful and beautiful fur. Bats can be black, brown, orange, silver-tipped, pale cream, even striped or spotted.

© Bats have **mammary glands** that make milk. A bat **pup** (a newborn bat) nurses at its mother's nipples to get milk. The pup lives on its mother's milk until it can hunt for its own food.

© Bats are **homeothermic**, or warm-blooded. They generate their own body heat and can keep their body temperatures warmer than their surroundings. But unlike most other mammals, bats can conserve energy by allowing their bodies to cool while they **roost** (rest) by day. This resting state is called **torpor**.

Bats are **not** birds.

© Bats do not have feathers or beaks.
© Bats do not build nests.
© Bats do not lay eggs.

Bats are **not** rodents.

© Bats belong in their own special group called Chiroptera, which is Greek for "hand wing."

© Bats are more closely related to humans and other **primates** (monkeys and apes) than they are to rodents like rats and mice.

Why Bat Has Short Legs

*L*ong ago, Killer-of-Enemies vowed to save his people from the terror of monster eagles that roamed the skies and carried off children. Killer-of-Enemies tricked one monster eagle into carrying him up to the eagle nest on the cliff, where he killed the monster eagle and its family. But Killer-of-Enemies did not know how to get down from the cliff. Just then, he saw an old woman approaching. It was Old Woman Bat.

"Grandmother, help me. Take me down," Killer-of-Enemies said.

Old Woman Bat looked all around, but did not see him. Killer-of-Enemies called again, and again, and again. Finally, Old Woman Bat saw him high in the eagle's nest. She came over to the cliff and began to climb.

"What are you doing here?" she asked, when she reached the top.

"Monster eagle carried me up here," he said. "Please take me down."

"Climb in my basket," Old Woman Bat said. Killer-of-Enemies looked at the burden basket on the old woman's back. Its carrying strap was made of spider's silk.

"That strap is too fine," he said. "It will break and I shall fall."

"Nonsense! I've carried a bighorn sheep in this basket," Old Woman Bat said. "Get in and close your eyes. If you look, we will fall."

Old Woman Bat clambered down the rock, singing a strange song. Her burden basket swayed wildly from side to side. Killer-of-Enemies thought the spider thread would surely break, so he opened his eyes to look.

As soon as Killer-of-Enemies opened his eyes, he and Old Woman Bat crashed down from the cliff. Old Woman Bat landed first and broke her legs. Killer-of-Enemies fell on top of her and was safe. Old Woman Bat's broken legs soon mended, but from that day on they have been short.

*Retold from a myth of the Chiricahua
Apache Indians of New Mexico*

Weird Knees

Bats have short back legs compared with their arms, hands, and fingers. Their knees are weird. They point backward or to the side. Their toes curl forward. The position of their knees and toes affects the way bats move about when they are not flying, as well as the way they roost.

Bats use their foot-claws and their thumbs to scramble along tree branches, cave walls, or even the ground. They can move very fast. You may see them crawling on all fours (their knees often stick out behind) or swinging by all fours, much as you might hang from a jungle gym. Most bats cannot walk upright. Unlike birds, their back legs are not very strong. Having weak back legs makes it tricky for bats to take to the air.

How do bats get a flying start? They hang head-down by their feet. Hanging upside down leaves the wings free to flap and gives the bat a starting lift. Then the bat lets go with its foot-claws and off it flies. Or the bat lets go with its foot-claws and drops for a while to gain enough speed to begin flying. Some bats <u>must</u> drop from a roost to begin their flight. They cannot launch from the ground.

Why Bat Has Wings

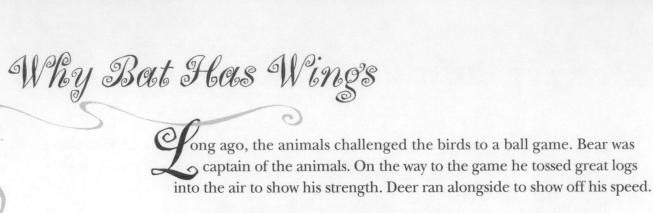

Long ago, the animals challenged the birds to a ball game. Bear was captain of the animals. On the way to the game he tossed great logs into the air to show his strength. Deer ran alongside to show off his speed.

Eagle was captain of the birds. Hawk and Falcon, both swift in flight, joined the team. But secretly, the birds were afraid the animals would win. The birds perched high in the trees, waiting for game time. Two furry things, not much larger than mice, scurried along a branch.

"Please, Eagle, let us play," they said.

"But you have four feet and fur. You belong with the animals," Eagle said.

"The animals would not have us," the furry things replied. "They said we were not strong or fast."

"To be on our team, you must have wings," Eagle said. So the birds took spare leather from a drumhead and cut two wing shapes from it. They stretched the leather shapes with cane splints and fastened them to the forelegs of the first little animal. In this way came *Tla'meha*, the bat. Eagle tossed the ball to him. He caught it in his wing and flew with it, dodging and circling. The birds knew he would do well on their team.

There was no more drum leather to make wings for the second animal.

"We'll have to stretch his skin," Eagle said. So the birds pulled at his fur with their beaks until the skin formed flaps between the little creature's front and hind legs. In this way came *Tewa*, the flying squirrel. He could carry the ball in his teeth as he glided from tree to tree.

The game began. Bat, skillful and agile, swooped close to the ground to catch the ball and carry it to the goal. He was the star player! The animals wished they had him on their team.

Retold from a legend of the
Cherokee Indians of Oklahoma

10

ACTIVITY: *Hand Wings*

One feature sets bats apart from all other mammals. Only bats have wings and can fly. Flying squirrels have flaps of skin, not wings. They glide instead of flapping to stay aloft.

All bats belong in the scientific order (group) Chiroptera. Discover why "hand wing" is such a good name for bats. Look at the bat skeleton on this page. Now hold the page up to the light. See how the bat body fits around its skeleton. Bat bones are thin and lightweight for flying.

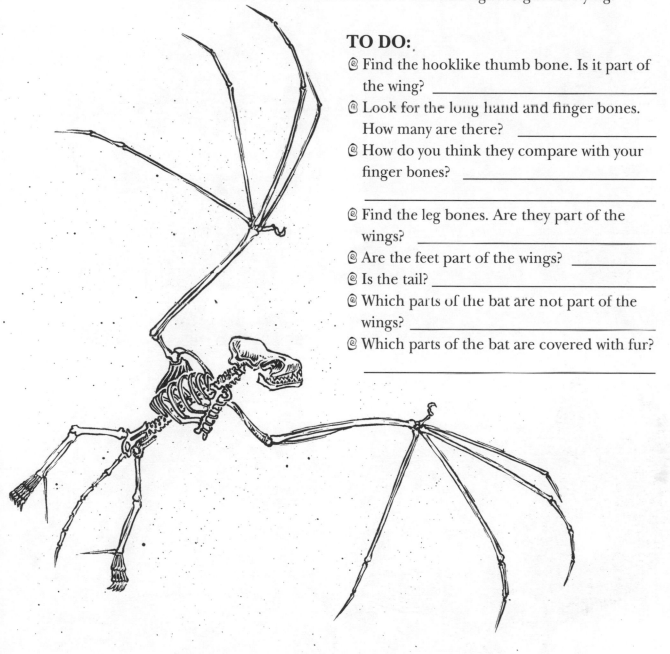

TO DO:

@ Find the hooklike thumb bone. Is it part of the wing? _____

@ Look for the long hand and finger bones. How many are there? _____

@ How do you think they compare with your finger bones? _____
_____

@ Find the leg bones. Are they part of the wings? _____

@ Are the feet part of the wings? _____

@ Is the tail? _____

@ Which parts of the bat are not part of the wings? _____

@ Which parts of the bat are covered with fur?
_____

Flight Check

You have seen how bat wings and bones fit together, but how do bat wings work? Bats curve or straighten their finger bones to change the shape of their wings for flight. Each wing can change shape independently to increase lift, help forward movement, or assist in making turns. Bats flap their wings using powerful muscles in their shoulders and chests, like a swimmer doing the butterfly stroke.

calcar

interfemoral
membrane

Not all bats have the same shape wings. Bats with long, thin wings are swift and direct in flight. Bats with short, wide wings flutter almost like butterflies. Stubby-winged bats don't go very far or fast, but they can turn in smaller spaces than the narrow-winged bats. They can hunt in dense woodlands.

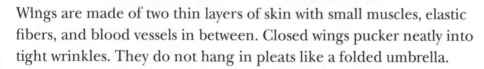

Wings are made of two thin layers of skin with small muscles, elastic fibers, and blood vessels in between. Closed wings pucker neatly into tight wrinkles. They do not hang in pleats like a folded umbrella.

Bat wings are often described as leathery, but don't imagine anything like shoe leather. Wings are about as thick as a plastic garbage bag or a rubber glove. Although wings are strong and tough, they sometimes puncture or tear. Luckily, small injuries heal quickly because of the large blood supply to the wings.

Some **species** (kinds) of bats have such transparent wings that you get an almost X-ray-type view of the bones.

The bat in the picture has an **interfemoral membrane** (tail membrane) that helps it fly. This membrane sometimes even acts as an insect-catcher. The bat flies with its back legs apart to keep the membrane stretched. The tail and the **calcar** (ankle spur) help keep the membrane tight. Not all bats have tail membranes. Not all bats have tails!

When it comes to landing, many bats do a quick flip in the air and grab their perch with their back feet. They roost with their heads pointing downward. This position seems upside down to us, perhaps, but the right way up for a bat. Do you think that to bats, we are the ones who are the wrong way up?

Hanging Out with Bats

Today, nearly 1,000 species of bats inhabit the world. They make up almost one quarter of all mammal species. They live everywhere except in Antarctica, the extreme northern tundra, some barren deserts, and a few islands. The tropics have the greatest **diversity** (number of species) of bats, but even the United States has 43 species.

So far, this book has talked about bats as if all bats were much the same. This fact is far from true. Although you can easily identify a bat as a bat by its body shape, species of bats are very different from one another. They vary in size, color, and body features; **habitats** (where they live); food choices; and in their family lives. A book like this one can only present a few of the hundreds of bat species to give you some idea of their amazing variety.

Before you meet some bats and find out what species they are, you will need to know some of the features that separate one species of bat from another.

Blind as a bat? Wrong! All bats can see well. The "true fruit bats," or flying foxes, form a subgroup of bats called Megachiroptera, or Megabats. They have large, doglike eyes. They use their eyes and their sense of smell to find flowers and fruit to eat. All other bats belong in a subgroup called Microchiroptera, or Microbats. They have small to very small eyes and most probably see only in black and white. They rely more on **echolocation** (listening to echoes to find objects) than vision to hunt for food and move around in the dark. (You might almost call echolocation "seeing with ears." Read more about echolocation on page 34.)

Ears come in an amazing variety of sizes and shapes. Some are simple and small. Others are large or enormous, with strange ridges and projections. Some ears have a **tragus**, a structure in the ear that sticks up like an ear within an ear. The tragus may be tall or short, wide or narrow, smooth or notched. Whatever the shape, a tragus helps direct echolocating calls into the ear.

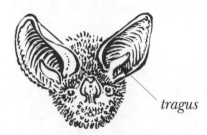

tragus

simple ear with no tragus

Noses are plain. Some have fleshy stand-up flaps called **nose leaves**. Nose leaves may be complex, with many folds and wrinkles.

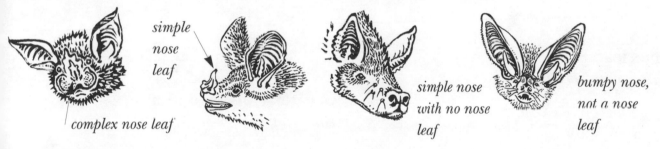

simple nose leaf

complex nose leaf

simple nose with no nose leaf

bumpy nose, not a nose leaf

Tails and tail membranes vary.

no tail

free tail

tail connected to interfemoral membrane

On the next two pages read about some bat species, then do the "Hanging Out with Bats" activity to find out what they look like.

X

Townsend's Big-eared Bat
Plecotus townsendii

Location: western North America from British Columbia to Mexico.

Appearance: light brown to slate gray color, enormous ears, large lumps at each side of snout.

Habitat: desert scrub, piñon-juniper and pine forests.

Life: roosts in mines, caves, or human-built structures; feeds on moths, beetles, and flies; hibernates in winter in small clusters with fur fuzzed up for insulation.

Tidbits: when at rest, these bats can coil their ears like ram's horns to conserve body heat.

American False Vampire
Vampyrum spectrum

Location: southern Mexico to Peru and central Brazil.

Appearance: largest New World bat; red-brown above, pale below.

Habitat: tropical forests and swamps in lowlands and foothills.

Life: up to five bats may roost together, usually in hollow trees; feeds on birds, rodents, frogs, insects, and fruit; may eat other bats, although this behavior has not been proven in the wild.

Tidbits: holds dead mice with its thumb claws, begins eating at head, and spits out tail; although "vampire" and "Vampyrum" appear in name, they do not feed on blood.

X

Straw-colored Fruit Bat
Eidolon helvum

Location: Africa south of Sahara, Saudi Arabia, and Madagascar.

Appearance: yellowish above and olive to brown below, appealing doglike face, ears twitch constantly as they monitor environment.

Habitat: tropical forests and savannahs.

Life: social, with colonies of up to a million bats; spends days in treetop roosts, where the colony is noisy and restless; feeds on ripe fruit and nectar from flowers; female has one baby a year, born after the rains, when fruit is plentiful.

Tidbits: One straw-colored fruit bat lived in a zoo over 21 years.

Greater Horseshoe Bat
Rhinolophus ferrumequinum

Location: southern Europe to Morocco, Afghanistan, and Japan.

Appearance: complicated horseshoe-shaped folds of skin surround nostrils; eyes small; ears large; broad, short wings cause fluttery flight.

Habitat: woodlands and open areas.

Life: eats insects; flies with mouth closed, emitting ultrasonic sounds through nostrils; nose leaf may help direct the sound beam; roosts in caves, hollow trees, foliage, or buildings.

Tidbits: often hunts from a favorite perch.

X

Spotted Bat
Euderma maculatum

Location: western United States and northern Mexico.

Appearance: three large white spots on the black fur of its back, pale wings, enormous pale ears.

Habitat: varied; but often dry, rough desert.

Life: roosts in cliff crevices, especially in places near water; eats moths and other insects caught in flight.

Tidbits: not easy to find or study, so scientists are not sure yet if it is rare, or even **endangered** (at risk of becoming extinct).

X

Frog-eating Bat
Trachops cirrhosus

Location: southern Mexico and Central America to Brazil.

Appearance: long nose with nose leaf, long ears.

Habitat: tropical forests.

Life: prey includes frogs; catches frogs by listening for their mating calls; avoids poisonous frogs by learning to recognize their particular calls.

Tidbits: frogs use shorter mating calls when frog-eating bats are flying, to reduce their chance of being overheard and eaten.

Fishing Bat
Noctilio leporinus

Location: Mexico to northern Argentina and Brazil, Cuba, and Jamaica.

Appearance: skin folds give "bulldog" look; long, slender ears with frilly traguses; long hind legs with large feet and sharp claws.

Habitat: rivers, streams, ponds, and coastlines.

Life: finds fish by echolocating fish fins that break the water surface; catches prey in forward-scooping claws; eats small fish in flight, larger prey at night roost; also eats aquatic insects.

Tidbits: if accidentally knocked into the water, can swim using wings as oars.

Pallid Bat
Antrozous pallidus

Location: western North America from British Columbia to Mexico.

Appearance: creamy yellow or light brown woolly fur, very large ridged ears, stubby nose.

Habitat: rocky outcrops, desert scrublands, woodlands.

Life: roosts in caves, mines, crevices, hollow trees, or buildings; catches prey on or near the ground; eats large moths, beetles, grasshoppers, crickets, centipedes, even scorpions; immune to centipede and scorpion stings.

Tidbits: most bats have single pups; pallid bats often have twins.

ACTIVITY: *Hanging Out with Bats*

Now it's time to find the bats and match each one to its description on page 16 or 17. When you are sure you know where each bat belongs, paste each bat above its description by its tab. When all the bats are in place, hold your open book face down and watch the bats hang out!

OBJECTIVE:
@ To identify the variety of bat species

THIS ACTIVITY INCLUDES:
@ Bat descriptions in "Hanging Out with Bats," pages 16 and 17
@ Hanging bat patterns on page 19
@ "Bat Key" on page 21
@ Answer key on page 64

YOU NEED:
@ Scissors
@ Paste, glue, or clear tape

BEFORE PLAYING:
@ Cut out all the bats on page 19 along the dashed lines.
@ Fold each tab along the solid line so the **X** is behind the bat's feet.

TO DO FIRST:
@ Select the ✱ bat. Follow these instructions step-by-step to learn how to use the "Bat Key" on page 21.
@ Read 1a and 1b of the "Bat Key," then look carefully at the ✱ bat. Does the ✱ bat have a nose leaf? No. Then choose 1b and GO TO 4.
@ Read 4a and 4b, then look at the ✱ bat again. Does the ✱ bat have large white spots? No. Choose 4b and GO TO 5.

@ Read 5a and 5b. Look at the ✱ bat. Does the bat have a tragus? Yes. Then choose 5a and GO TO 6.
@ Read 6a and 6b. Look at your bat. Is the tragus frilly? No. Is the lip bulldog-like? No. So choose 6b and GO TO 7.
@ Read 7a and 7b. Measure the ✱ bat's ears using the scale. Are they longer than the arrows? No. Is the nose lumpy at the side? No. Then choose 7b which tells you your bat is a pallid bat.
@ Find the pallid bat's description on page 17. Match the **X** on the tab behind the bat's feet to the **X** above the description. Use a dab of paste, a drop of glue, or a small piece of tape to attach only the tab to the **X** on the page. The bat picture should be facing up.

TO DO NEXT:
@ Use the "Bat Key" to identify each bat in turn. Start at 1a in the key every time you start with a new bat.
@ As you identify the bats, paste them above their descriptions on page 16 or 17.

AFTER PLAYING:
@ When all the bats are in place and the paste or glue is dry, turn to pages 16 and 17. Hold the pages open and turn the book face down to watch the bats hang out.

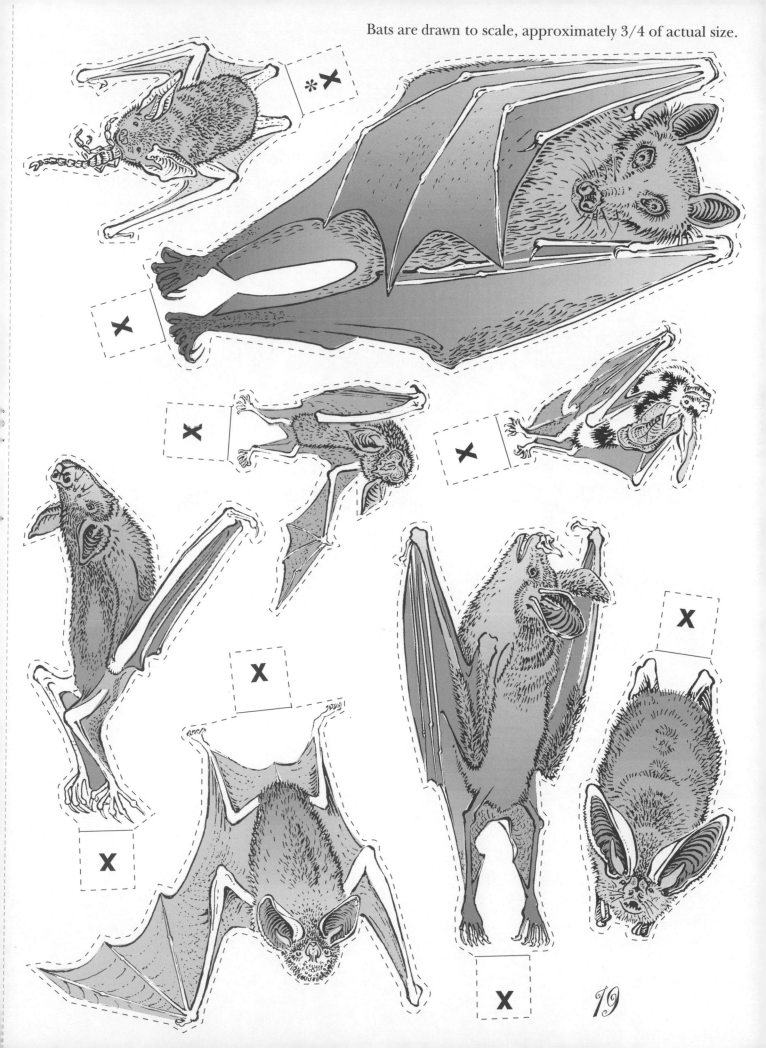

Bats are drawn to scale, approximately 3/4 of actual size.

19

20

BAT KEY

Keys are found in many field guides. They are designed to help identify an animal new to you. Read the first two statements of the key carefully. Next, look closely at the features of your animal. Then decide which statement in the key best describes your animal. The choice you make will either tell you what to read next, or will tell you the name of the animal.

1a. Nose with leaf-shaped projection (nose leaf),
☞ **GO TO 2.**

1b. Nose without nose leaf,
☞ **GO TO 4.**

2a. Nose leaf complex and U-shaped.
❀ **GREATER HORSESHOE BAT**

2b. Nose leaf simple, not U-shaped,
☞ **GO TO 3.**

3a. Long snout and no tail.
❀ **AMERICAN FALSE VAMPIRE**

3b. Shorter snout with fringed lips, tail.
❀ **FROG-EATING BAT**

4a. Large white spots on back.
❀ **SPOTTED BAT**

4b. No large white spots on back,
☞ **GO TO 5.**

5a. Ears with tragus (projection inside ear),
☞ **GO TO 6.**

5b. Ears without tragus, eyes quite large.
❀ **STRAW-COLORED FRUIT BAT**

6a. Tragus frilly, split front lip bulldog-like.
❀ **FISHING BAT**

6b. Tragus not frilly, front lip not split,
☞ **GO TO 7.**

7a. Nose with side lumps, ears shorter than the arrows on scale.
❀ **TOWNSEND'S BIG-EARED BAT**

7b. Stub-nose with no lumps, ridged ears longer than the arrows on scale.
❀ **PALLID BAT**

SCALE
Measure ears here

Why Bat Hangs Upside Down

Once, long ago, Coyote thought he would take a wife, but did not know whom to choose.

"Why not take the wife of Hawk Chief?" Bat said, for Hawk Chief was missing, and had not been seen for many days.

But Hawk Chief returned and became angry with Bat for giving such ill-considered advice. He picked Bat up and slung him with full force into a juniper bush. Bat hung upside down in the bush, caught by his long, pointy-toed moccasins. He twisted and he turned, but however much he struggled, he could not get free. And from that time on bats hang upside down—even when they sleep.

*Retold from a myth of the
Lipan Apache Indians of Texas*

Bats spend most of their nonflying time upside down—eating, sleeping, and grooming. In their upside down life they can find places to roost that most other animals cannot use. Upside down, they are always ready for a flying start.

You may wonder if bats ever get tired just hanging around, and fall from their roosts. The answer is no. A special arrangement of tendons in a bat's legs and claws prevents it from falling. The weight of the hanging bat tightens its grip. Bats cling while they sleep. Even dead bats have been found still hanging from their roosts.

While a bat is sleeping or inactive, its body functions slow down and its temperature drops. The bat saves energy, needs less food, and so needs to hunt less often. Scientists wonder if this inactivity prevents wear and tear on bat bodies, helping them live longer. If bats survive their first year, they may live between 5 and 10 years, or even as many as 20 or 30 years! This is much longer than most other small mammals, such as mice, which may only live about a year.

When bats are not eating or sleeping, they spend time grooming—upside down. Many people believe that bats are dirty. These people are wrong. Bats are very fussy about personal hygiene. They groom themselves much the way cats and dogs do, using their tongues and the claws on their feet. They hold on with one foot while grooming with the other. Some even clean their teeth with their claws. Every inch of each wing, inside and out, gets a thorough grooming to keep it in good flying condition. Oil from special glands is used to keep the wings soft and flexible. (You will know how this works if you have ever oiled a baseball glove.)

Pups in the Cave

Imagine a nursery with millions of babies all wanting attention. . . no, not human babies! This is a nursery for Mexican free-tailed bat pups—in a place like Carlsbad Cavern.

Carlsbad Cavern in New Mexico houses one of the most famous bat maternity roosts in the United States. Hundreds of thousands of Mexican free-tailed bats and smaller numbers of several other species of bats use the cave, generally from mid-April through mid-October. At night, the bats fly out in great columns to hunt for insects—and that is probably how the cave was discovered. The first people to discover the natural entrance of Carlsbad Caverns did so centuries ago. These prehistoric tribes probably used the natural entrance as shelter. At least ten range wanderers, from 1880–1905, have claimed to be the first to discover Carlsbad Caverns. Historians cannot say who was first. Whoever it was probably saw what looked like a thick plume of smoke spiraling into the air. The "smoke" was really millions of bats rising from an opening in the ground. Carlsbad Caverns National Park protects this famous bat cavern. Visit this park in summer and watch in the early evening as huge numbers of bats take flight—looking like a twirling ribbon or the funnel cloud of a tornado.

Mexican free-tailed bats spend the winter in Mexico. Male and female bats mate in February or March. After mating, the males do not share in raising a family. The bats return to Carlsbad Cavern and other caves and roosts in the southwestern United States in late spring and the females have their young.

The largest known nursery colony (Bracken Cave in Texas) has about 20 million bats in residence. This rates as the highest density of mammals that ever gathers in one place. (They are good neighbors and pest-controllers, eating about a quarter of a million tons of insects in just one night!)

Bat Pup Facts

- Mexican free-tailed bat nursery caves are dark and warm from all the huddled bodies. They may smell of ammonia from urine.
- Most young are born within two weeks in June. Each mother has one pup.
- Pups are born feet first. The mother's tail and wing membranes form a safety net during birth. The pup then crawls up the mother's fur, finds a nipple, and begins to suckle.
- Newborn pups are pink and hairless. They have open eyes and small wings.
- A mother bat can fly with her pup holding onto her fur. But bat pups are usually left in the nursery while their mothers hunt.
- A female returns to feed her own pup about twice a day. She remembers where she left her pup hanging. But, if her pup has moved, she finds it among the crowd by its unique calls and smell.
- Free-tailed pups are ready to fly and hunt at about five weeks old.
- Some free-tailed bat pups fall from their roosts or crash during flight practice. The mother bat cannot rescue the pup—she is unable to fly down, pick up the pup, and take off again from the ground. The pups do not survive long. They may be eaten by raccoons, skunks, or weasels. They may have their bones picked clean by dermestid beetles that live on the cave floor.
- Life outside is dangerous, too. Owls, snakes, or hawks may be on the prowl.
- By August, adults and young fly out each night to hunt. You can see bat "smoke" plumes against the sky.

Only a few kinds of bats have more than one pup. Big brown bats and pallid bats may have two. Red bats sometimes have four. But single-pup families are the standard. It is unusual that such small mammals should have only a single offspring. (Think of mice having nests full of eight or more young.)

Bats make up for having small families, because they live long lives and have one pup a year for many years. When nature is in balance, this behavior works well. But if anything happens to reduce a bat population, it takes much longer for the population to build up again. Bats that live in caves are especially at risk. One destructive act by humans (vandalism), or one natural disaster such as a flood, can wipe out huge numbers of bats at the same time, putting the survival of that species at risk.

Not all bats gather in enormous colonies to have their young. Some species have their young in much smaller colonies in caves, mines, hollow trees, or even human dwellings—either abandoned or occupied. Bat nursery colonies are noisy places, with much squeaking and squabbling. In fact, hearing bat sounds is often the first clue people have that they are sharing their homes with bats. It is not necessarily bad to have bats in your house—in fact many people would be honored! However, if too many bats become noisy or messy neighbors, you can remove the bats without harming them. Contact your local Wildlife Service for more information.

ACTIVITY: *Pups in the Cave*

OBJECTIVE:

◎ To build a three-dimensional bat cave

THIS ACTIVITY INCLUDES:

◎ The bat cave scene on page 29
◎ The bat cave cutouts on page 31

YOU NEED:

◎ Scissors
◎ A pencil (it will be easier to cut out the cave entrance if you poke a hole with the pencil first)
◎ Crayons or colored pencils
◎ Paste or glue

BEFORE ASSEMBLING:

◎ Color the scenery on page 29 and the cave pieces on page 31 before you cut them out.
◎ Cut out the hole for the cave entrance on page 29 along the dashed line. DO NOT remove the page from the book!
◎ Remove page 31 from the book by cutting along the dashed line. Cut out the background pieces, the **stalactites** (formations that hang down from a cave's ceiling), and the bats along the dashed lines. DO NOT cut any solid lines!

TO ASSEMBLE:

◎ Follow the directions on page 28 to build the pop-up bat cave background.

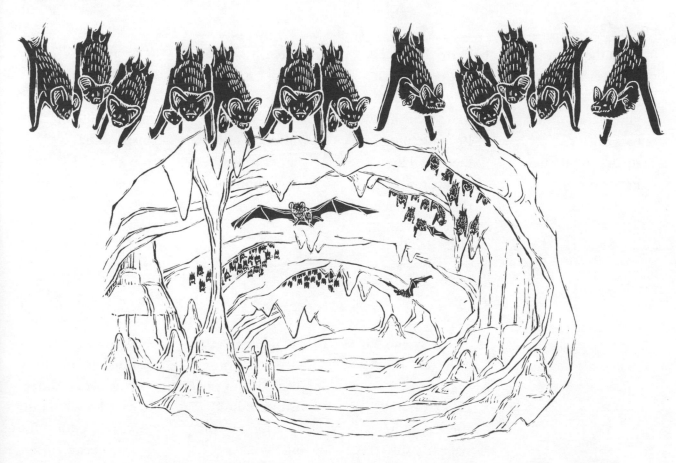

HOW TO BUILD A BAT CAVE

1. With the cave background picture facing up, fold the left side panel over the picture along the solid line.

2. Fold the strip along the solid line so the **X**s face up.

3. Do the same to the right side. Your cave background should look like this.

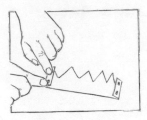

4. With the stalactite pictures face down, fold along the solid lines to make tabs, the letters facing up.

5. Turn the stalactite pictures face up. With just a dab of glue, paste some bats onto each stalactite picture, heads down!

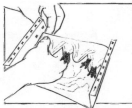

6. Paste the tabs **A** to the **A**s on the side panels. Match the arrows. Both pictures face up. The stalactites hang down.

7. Paste the tabs **B** to the **B**s on the side panels. Match the arrows. These stalactites will be higher so you can see behind them.

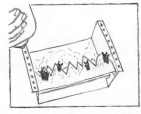

8. Your cave background is complete. Put a little glue on the strips marked with the **X**s to paste it into the book.

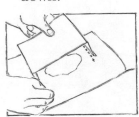

9. Turn to page 30 and paste the **X**s on the cave background to the **X**s on the page. Be sure the arrows point the same way.

10. Turn back to the cave scene on page 29 and peek through the opening to view the three-dimensional bat cave.

11. When you are finished and the glue is dry, the cave background will fold down flat so you can close your book.

DO NOT CUT OUT
THIS PAGE!
This page stays in
the book. Cut only
the dashed line
to make this the
cave opening.

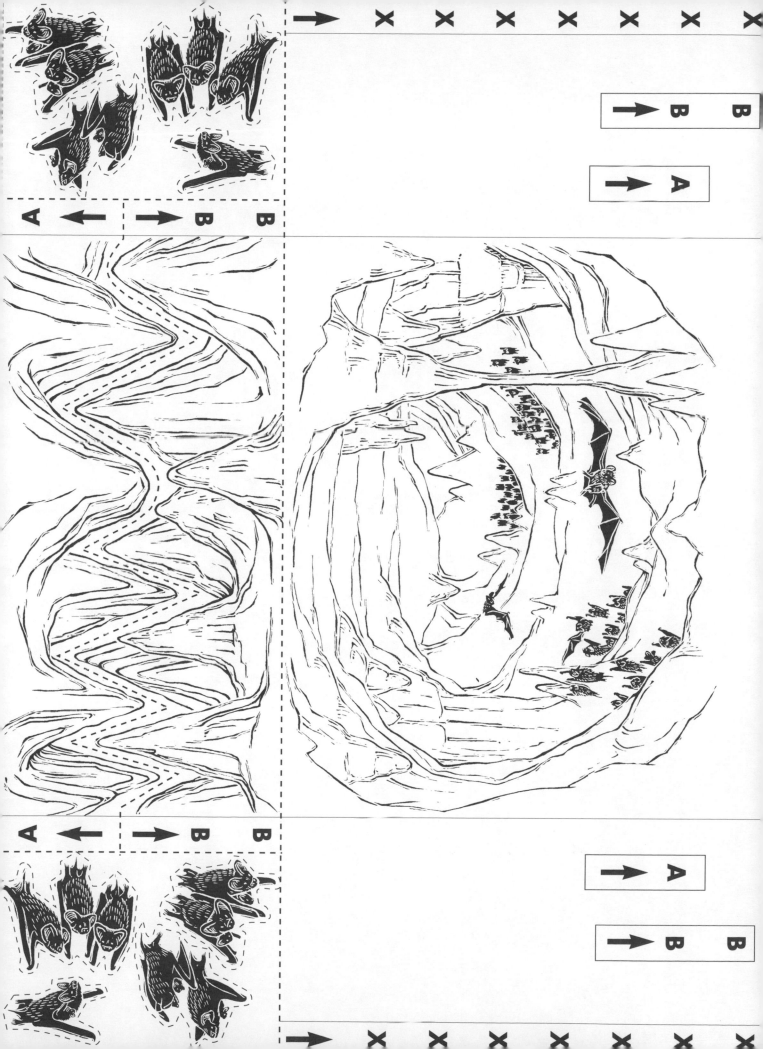

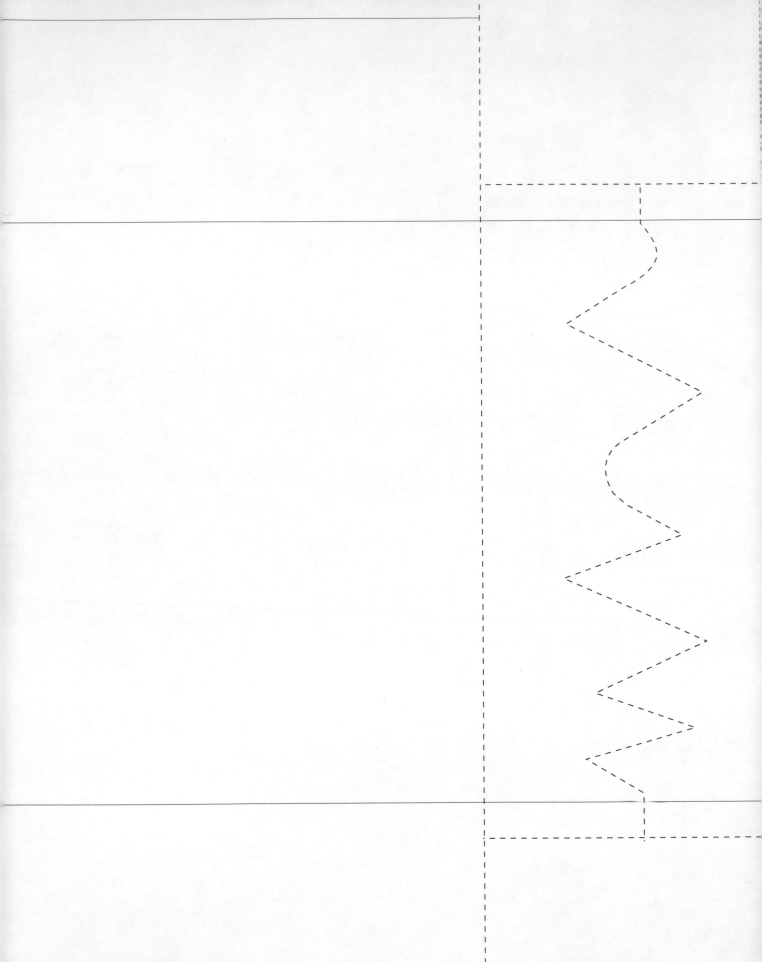

32

Why Bat Flies at Night

*L*ong ago, when first the world was made, it never became dark or cold. All day the sun shone brightly, giving creatures warmth and light. All night the full moon gleamed, making twilight almost as light as day. Until . . .

One day, Bat accepted a mission to carry a mysterious basket to the moon. In the basket was darkness, but Bat did not know that.

Bat took off to fly to the moon with the basket on his back.

"Bother this basket," he said after a while. "It is too heavy and I am tired and hungry." So Bat put the basket down and went to find some food and take a rest.

Along came some other animals. They saw the basket abandoned along the way.

"That is a large basket," said one of them. "I wonder if it is full of good things to eat?"

"Let's open it and see," said another.

Just as the animals were peeking under the basket lid, Bat came back. But he was too late. Darkness had escaped.

Ever since that time, Bat rests by day so he is ready to fly at twilight. At night, you will see him rushing about everywhere. He is trying to catch all the pieces of dark to put back in the basket, so he can take it to the moon. His mission now is to capture every tatter of darkness.

Retold from a legend of the Kono people
of Sierra Leone, Africa

Shapes in the Night Sky

Bats are **nocturnal**. They are active at night, and sleep by day. They spend the nights hunting. No matter how dark the night, bats fly around without bumping into objects or each other. Many of them catch tiny insects and eat them as they fly. How's that for fast food? It is all done by echolocation—the use of echoes to locate objects.

Bats send **pulses** (beeps) of sound through the air. The pulses hit an object and bounce back as echoes. The bat hears the echoes and its brain works out a sound picture of the object. The bat can tell if the object is moving prey or a fixed part of the landscape.

Most bat beeps are **ultrasonic** (high-pitched) and above the range of human hearing. Some bat beeps are within human hearing range. Children have more acute hearing than adults. (Why not take your parents bat-hunting? You may hear bats when your parents cannot!) If we *could* hear all bat pulses, a night walk might deafen us, with bat sounds as loud as jackhammers.

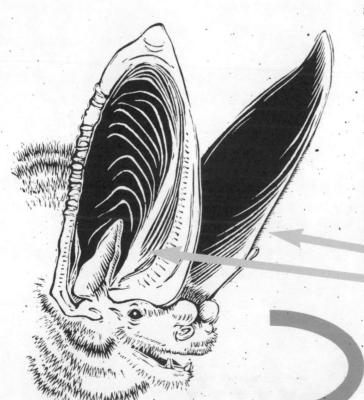

A bat makes sound with its **larynx** (voice box) as we do. Some bats beep through their mouths. Others beep through their noses. During each beep, a special muscle contracts in the bat's ears to stop it from being deafened by its own voice. A hunting or cruising bat sends out ten or twenty beeps a second and listens for returning echoes. When it finds prey, perhaps an insect, a bat beeps faster so more echo information bounces back. The bat figures how large the insect is, how far away it is, how fast it is traveling, and in which direction—all in a fraction of a second. That's impressive computing!

The bat homes in on its prey. Zap! It catches the insect in its mouth, wing, or tail membrane. If the insect is small, the bat eats it right away. If the insect is large, the bat carries it back to a nearby night roost, flips over, and hangs up to eat. You may wonder how a bat holds a large insect without dropping it. Thumb claws make excellent dining tools. Bats discard hard parts. Sometimes piles of moth wings collect beneath bat roosts—signs of successful hunting.

If a bat can catch a gnat by echolocation, do you honestly believe a bat would fly into your hair? It is not likely.

The strange ears and weird nose leaves that some bats have help echolocation. They channel echoes coming in or sound going out. These flaps and folds look strange to us; some people may even think they make the bats ugly. But to the bats that have them, the flaps and folds are essential. Besides, to another bat of the same species, the flaps and folds might look beautiful! Who are we to judge?

Only one small group of Megabats have echolocation. They make audible clicks with their tongues. They use echolocation to get around in the caves where they roost. Once outside, they rely on their eyes. They, like all the rest of the Megabats, see well enough in the dark to find food. Besides, they don't have to pursue moving food . . . fruit stays put!

Eavesdropping

Some moths eavesdrop to escape being eaten. The moths can hear ultrasonic bat pulses with special hearing structures on their bodies. If the sounds are fairly quiet, the moth changes its flight path to move out of the way. If the sounds are loud, indicating the bat is dangerously close, the moth closes its wings and drops to the ground out of harm's way.

Tiger moths don't just eavesdrop, they answer back. They make clicking sounds that resemble ultrasonic bat calls. Perhaps the clicks confuse the bat's echolocation. Perhaps the bat thinks there is another bat nearby. Or the trick may be more complicated. Tiger moths taste horrible. In daylight their bright colors serve as a warning to predators to leave them alone; they are not good to eat. But their bright, warning colors are no help in the dark. Instead, the tiger moth's clicks are an active warning for bats to leave them alone.

ACTIVITY: *A~Mazing Appetites*

You might wonder if bats fly nonstop and take the shortest way from place to place. This behavior might be true sometimes, but certainly not when they are seeking food. Bats zigzag in all directions as they hunt.

Suppose you are a bat on your nightly hunt. Fly through the maze of obstacles, using your echolocation, and count up all the insects you manage to catch on the way back to your cave.

OBJECTIVE:
@ To fly from your night roost above the chair to the bat cave at the top of the picture, <u>and</u> catch enough food to eat on the way. You need 100 or more food points or you will go to bed hungry!

THIS ACTIVITY INCLUDES:
@ The scorecard on this page
@ The maze on the next page

YOU NEED:
@ A pencil

TO DO:
@ Begin at the night roost and mark your flight path through the maze using your echolocation pencil.
@ Keep score by the food value of what you catch. Mosquitoes=1, beetles=5, moths=10. You need 100 or more food points or you go to the cave hungry!
@ You may have to forage along several paths to find the one that gives you enough food, so mark a path lightly so you can erase it if you must. Keep trying until you find a route that satisfies your appetite! Then you can mark it in darker pencil.

KEY

Moth=10 points

Beetle=5 points

Mosquito=1 point

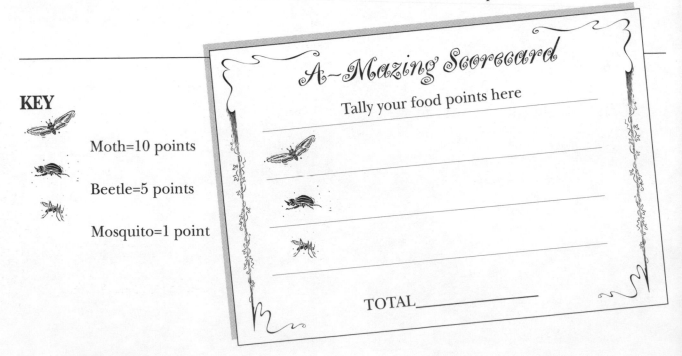

A~Mazing Scorecard
Tally your food points here

TOTAL _____

BAT CAVE

NIGHT
ROOST

37

ACTIVITY: *The Night Shift*

You may wonder why bats evolved a skill as complicated as echolocation just so they could hunt at night. After all, they have perfectly good eyes. Why don't they just hunt by day?

One answer is that by being nocturnal, bats have the night-flying insects almost to themselves. They have very little competition for a great food resource. If bats hunted by day, they would compete with hundreds of kinds of insect-eating birds. Another answer is that by hunting in the dark and hiding away in concealed roosts by day, bats reduce their risk of being caught by **predators** (animals that hunt and kill other animals for food).

OBJECTIVE:

@ To construct your "Day Shift/Night Shift" wheel to see how a **riparian** (riverbank) habitat might change from day to night. At the same time you will be building the "Wheel-O-Meal" on the back.

THIS ACTIVITY INCLUDES:

@ The riparian habitat picture on page 39
@ The "Day Shift/Night Shift" key on page 39
@ The "Wheel-O-Meal" game on page 40, which shows what bats eat
@ The "Day Shift-Night/Shift Wheel" on page 41 and the "Wheel-O-Meal Wheel" on page 42

YOU NEED:

@ Scissors
@ A pencil (it will be easier to cut out the circles if you poke a hole with the pencil first)
@ A 3/4-inch brad (also called a paper fastener)

TO DO:

@ Follow the dashed lines to cut out the blank circles on page 39. Poke with a pencil (CAREFUL!) to start your cuts without damaging the surrounding picture. Cut along the dashed lines at the top of the picture to make a flap.
@ Next, cut out the "Day Shift/Night Shift Wheel" from page 41. Behind it on page 42 is the "Wheel-O-Meal Wheel" which you are cutting out at the same time.
@ Fasten the wheel with the type side up on page 40 by placing a brad through both **X** marks. Place the flap at the top of the page over the wheel.
@ Turn back to page 39. Turn the wheel at the top of the page to observe the changes in the riparian habitat. The moon identifies the night shift, the sun the day shift.

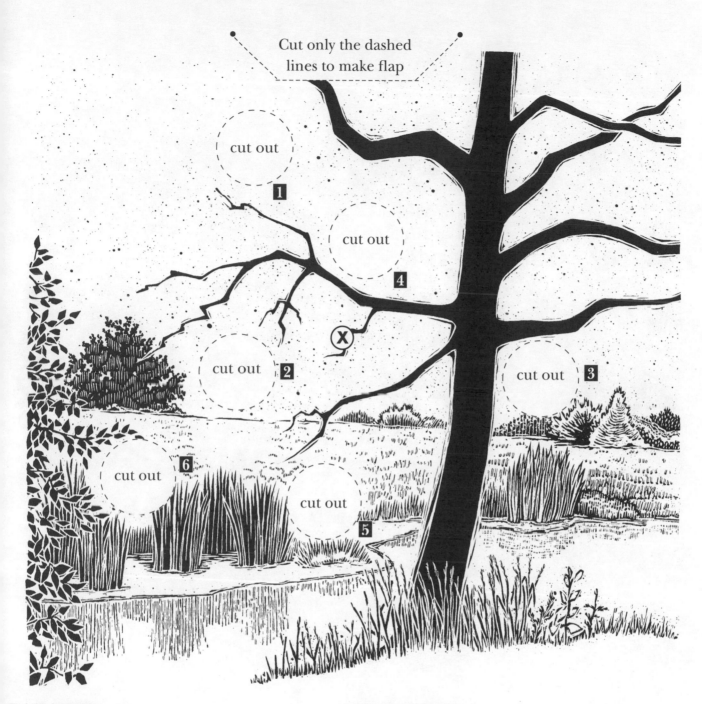

Cut only the dashed lines to make flap

cut out **1**

cut out **4**

cut out **2**

cut out **3**

Ⓧ

cut out **6**

cut out **5**

DAY SHIFT

1. Bats rest, socialize, and groom during the day.
2. Swallows are daylight **insectivores** (insect eaters).
3. Many birds **glean** (collect) insects in the trees.
4. Hawks may catch bats that fly in early evening.
5. Many birds hunt butterflies.
6. Some bats roost among leaves by day.

NIGHT SHIFT

1. Bats avoid hunting at full moon to avoid predators.
2. Bats hunt unless it is cold, windy, or raining.
3. Some bats return to a night roost to eat.
4. Owls may prey on bats when they can catch them.
5. Many bats relish a juicy moth abdomen for dinner.
6. Some bats **glean** (collect) insects from bark and leaves.

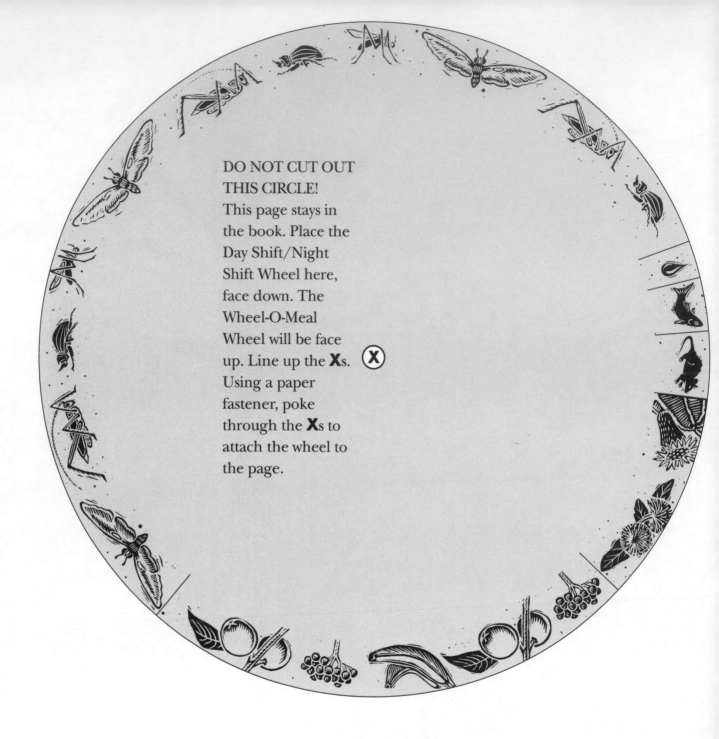

DO NOT CUT OUT
THIS CIRCLE!
This page stays in
the book. Place the
Day Shift/Night
Shift Wheel here,
face down. The
Wheel-O-Meal
Wheel will be face
up. Line up the **X**s. Ⓧ
Using a paper
fastener, poke
through the **X**s to
attach the wheel to
the page.

ACTIVITY: *Wheel~O~Meal*

TO DO:

◎ Turn the "Wheel-O-Meal Wheel" until the lines on the wheel match
the lines around the edge. See how many kinds of bats eat each kind
of food.

Cut out this circle along the dashed line.

DAY SHIFT/NIGHT SHIFT WHEEL

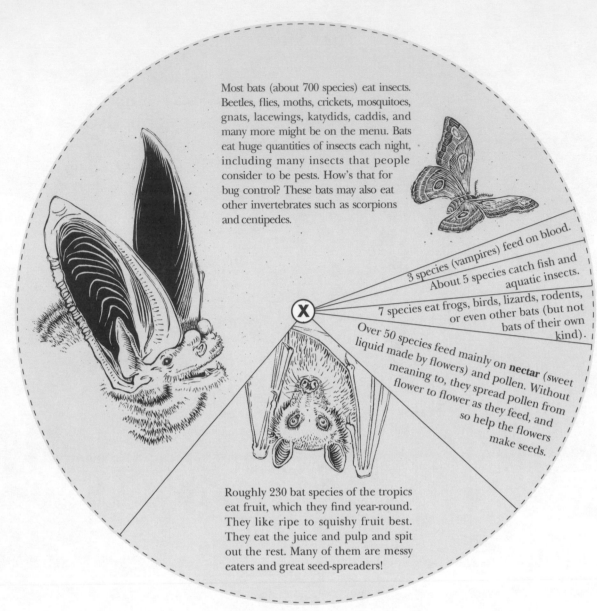

Most bats (about 700 species) eat insects. Beetles, flies, moths, crickets, mosquitoes, gnats, lacewings, katydids, caddis, and many more might be on the menu. Bats eat huge quantities of insects each night, including many insects that people consider to be pests. How's that for bug control? These bats may also eat other invertebrates such as scorpions and centipedes.

3 species (vampires) feed on blood.

About 5 species catch fish and aquatic insects.

7 species eat frogs, birds, lizards, rodents, or even other bats (but not bats of their own kind).

Over 50 species feed mainly on **nectar** (sweet liquid made by flowers) and pollen. Without meaning to, they spread pollen from flower to flower as they feed, and so help the flowers make seeds.

Roughly 230 bat species of the tropics eat fruit, which they find year-round. They like ripe to squishy fruit best. They eat the juice and pulp and spit out the rest. Many of them are messy eaters and great seed-spreaders!

Cut out this circle along the dashed line.

WHEEL-O-MEAL WHEEL

Batty Choices

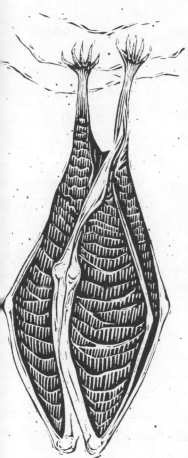

Bats that live in the tropics can find food all year. However, insects, fruit, pollen, and nectar may be scarce at times, especially during dry periods. The bats may have to travel to different areas to feed. But then the rains come, and plenty of food is again available.

Life is not so easy for insect-eating bats in colder climates. During winter, insects are few, or gone entirely. Bats could **migrate** (travel) to a warmer, insect-rich area. They could **hibernate** (spend the winter in an inactive state) until insects return in spring. Either choice has its problems and perils.

If bats migrate, they must . . .

- Store fat to fuel a long journey.
- Not get lost on the journey. Bats use their eyes to navigate by landmarks, because echolocation works only at short-range.
- Travel up to 1,000 miles (1,600 km) or more, surviving storms and other dangers.
- Find roosts on arrival, usually ones they traditionally occupy.
- Find enough food in the winter habitat.
- Maybe risk being mistaken for vampire bats, and killed.
- Make the same dangerous journey in reverse next year.

Do Not Disturb!

Bats lose up to one-third or more of their body weight by the end of hibernation and have little or no fat reserves left. Any time a bat is roused, it uses energy to warm up and become alert—precious energy that should have lasted for one or two months more of sleep. This activity leaves the bat with little margin of safety—its fuel may run out before spring.

Bats should never be disturbed while they hibernate. It could be their death sentence.

If bats hibernate, they must . . .

- Store sufficient fat to survive winter, however long and harsh.
- Possibly travel 30 to 300 miles to find a cave, mine, building, hollow tree, or other shelter with good roosts.
- Check that the site is not too cold (they could freeze), too warm (they would use energy too fast), or too dry (they need humid air).
- Risk spring coming late; their fat-fuel might run out.
- Risk being roused by humans, wasting energy needed for survival.
- Risk being forced out or killed by vandals.

No Bats, No Bananas

Across the tropical and subtropical parts of the world, flying foxes and other fruit bats not only eat fruit, they also grow it! Here's how they become gardeners.

Some bats carry pollen from one flower to another, even though they don't do so on purpose. These bats are nectar-sippers, like hummingbirds. As they push their snouts into a flower to lap nectar with their long, pointed tongues, they get dusted with pollen. Some pollen rubs off inside the next flower they visit and fertilizes it to make seeds. Other pollen is eaten by the bats as they groom their fur. To the bats, pollen tastes good and is nutritious. To the plants, pollen is essential to seed production. If it were not for these bats spreading pollen, many plants would not survive. In other words there's a risk: no bats . . . maybe no baobabs and no wild bananas.

Bats also eat fruit—lots of it—bananas, mangoes, guavas, figs, and other fruits and berries, large and small. Some bats are messy eaters, spilling as they slurp. They spit out stringy fruit and skin. They digest meals in just fifteen to twenty minutes, then **defecate** (poop) as they fly, spreading undigested seeds over the ground below. The seeds that the bats spread on clear-cut areas are especially important. Many of those seeds, deposited with a helpful shot of fertilizer, grow into tomorrow's forests. Bats planted them.

44

Without the baobab—the African tree of life—many animals, from hornbills and bushbabies to honeybees and pythons, would be without home and food. In times of drought, even elephants eat baobab trunks for the water they contain. Yet the tree depends on bats, like the Egyptian fruit bat, for pollination to grow the baobab trees of the future.

Without saguaro cactus, organ pipe cactus, and agave plants, the deserts of the American Southwest could not sustain all the other creatures—from elf owls to antelope ground squirrels—that depend on the plants for shelter and food. Yet without the lesser long-nosed bat, these desert plants lose a vital nighttime pollinator.

Bats like these are sometimes described as **keystone species**—their loss may cause a whole ecosystem to come tumbling down.

No living things live in isolation. Each one depends on many others for survival. Bats need plants for fruit, nectar, and pollen. Plants need bats for pollination and seed-scattering. Lose one, risk losing all—it's as simple as that.

ACTIVITY: *Flick and Fly*

Did you ever wish you could take a closer look at the swift shadows of the twilight? Make a flick book and see the motion of the bat's wings as they move across the night sky.

OBJECTIVE:
@ To construct your own flick book to observe bats in flight.

THIS ACTIVITY INCLUDES:
@ The "Flying Bat Illustrations" (the pages for your book) on pages 47 and 49

YOU NEED:
@ Scissors
@ A stapler

TO DO:
@ Remove the next two pages along the dashed lines. One by one, cut these pages into mini-pages along the dashed lines.
@ Arrange your pages <u>by number</u> (page 1 on top, then page 2, page 3, etc.) with the bat picture sides up. You will notice type upside down on the other side of the pages.
@ Staple your book at the **X** marks. Now you are ready to flick and fly.
@ Hold the book by the stapled end and flip the pages quickly to observe a bat in flight.

AFTER PLAYING:
@ Keep your book and flip it over to play the "Twenty Questions" game.

ACTIVITY: *Twenty Questions*

The print side of your "Flick and Fly" book contains a special Bat-O-Gram, a message about bats. It is hidden among all the facts in the flick book, in code, and needs solving!

OBJECTIVE:
@ To try the "Twenty Questions" quiz.
@ To solve the "Bat-O-Gram" as you check your answers.

THE GAME INCLUDES:
@ Your "Flick and Fly" bat flick book
@ Twenty true (T) or false (F) statements and the "Bat-O-Gram" on page 51
@ The Answer Key on page 64

YOU NEED:
@ A pencil

TO DO:
@ Mark true (T) or false (F) in the space before each statement in the quiz.
@ Read the "Bat Facts" side of your book to check your answers.
@ Score one point each time you answered true or false correctly.
@ Each page that gives an answer also has one shaded letter.
@ Write the shaded letter from the answer in the box following the quiz statement it explains.
@ Copy the letters in order in the "Bat-O-Gram" blanks below the quiz and the message will be revealed!

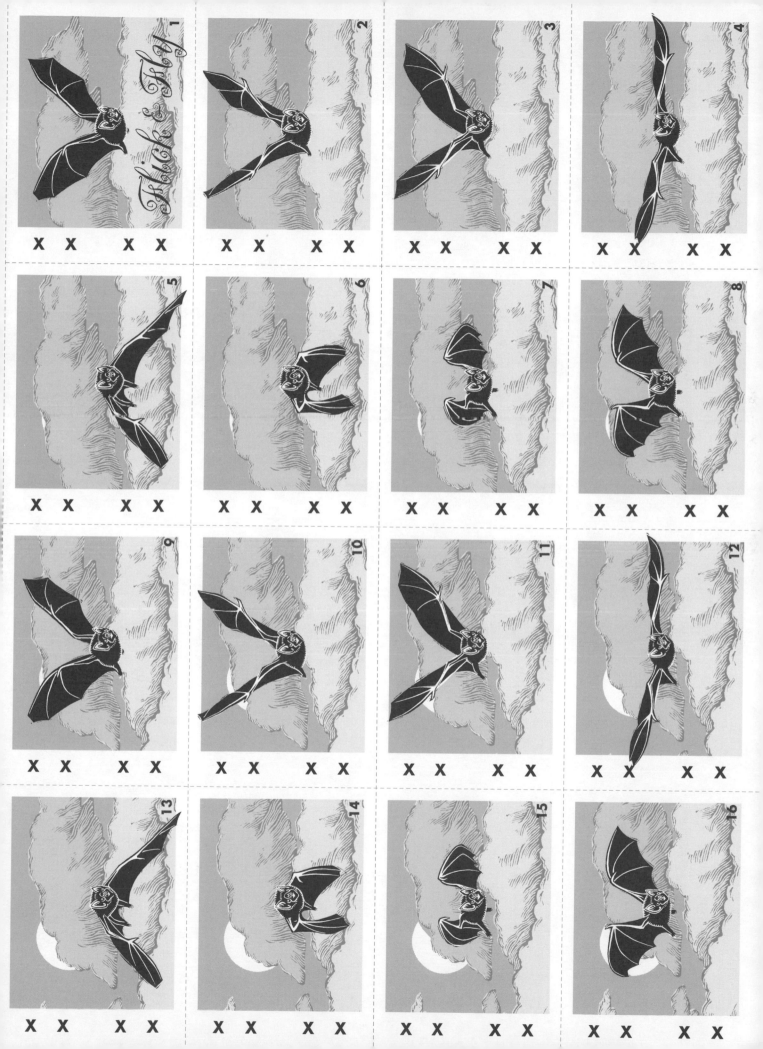

One advantage of roosting upside down from cave ceilings is that bats are out of the way of many predators.

Bats have good vision. Migrating bats navigate using their eyes to see geographical landmarks. Echolocation is only a short-range tool.

Bats can be found everywhere in the world except Antarctica and a few islands.

Like all mammal **s**, bats have fur that helps keep them warm.

Many bats that roost in trees are camouflaged. With their wings wrapped around them, they look like dead leaves.

Some little brown bats, *Myotis lucifugus* (North America), are known to have lived more than 30 years in the wild.

A bat pup is l**i**ve-born. Immediately after birth, the pup clambers up its mother's fur and suckles at her nipple.

Some research suggests Megabats may be our distant relatives. Their brains have some features similar to primate brains.

Fruit-eating bats eat up to three times their own body weight in a night. (That is like a 10-year-old child eating about 500 or 600 hamburgers!)

The wrinkle-faced **b**at, *Centurio senex* (Mexico and Central America), has a chin flap with built-in transparent eye-windows that are pulled over its face and eyes when it sleeps.

A short-tailed fruit bat, *Carollia perspicillata* (Central to South America), can scatter 60,000 seeds in a single night and aids forest regrowth.

Each kind of bat has its own hunting call. Scientists can learn to recognize species by using electronic bat-detectors to listen to the patterns of bat calls.

Mother bats recognize their own babies from the crowd in the cave by voic**e** and smell.

Male hammer-headed bats, *Hypsignathus monstrosus* (Gambia, Ethiopia, Zambia), gather in leks (courting grounds) and call loudly. The best honker **g**ets the most mates.

Forty-three species of bats live in the United States. Six species are listed as endangered (at risk of becoming extinct). Many more are being considered for endangered listing.

Most bats have a single baby in a year. The pup is born as its mother han**g**s from a roost. Bats make no kind of nest or den.

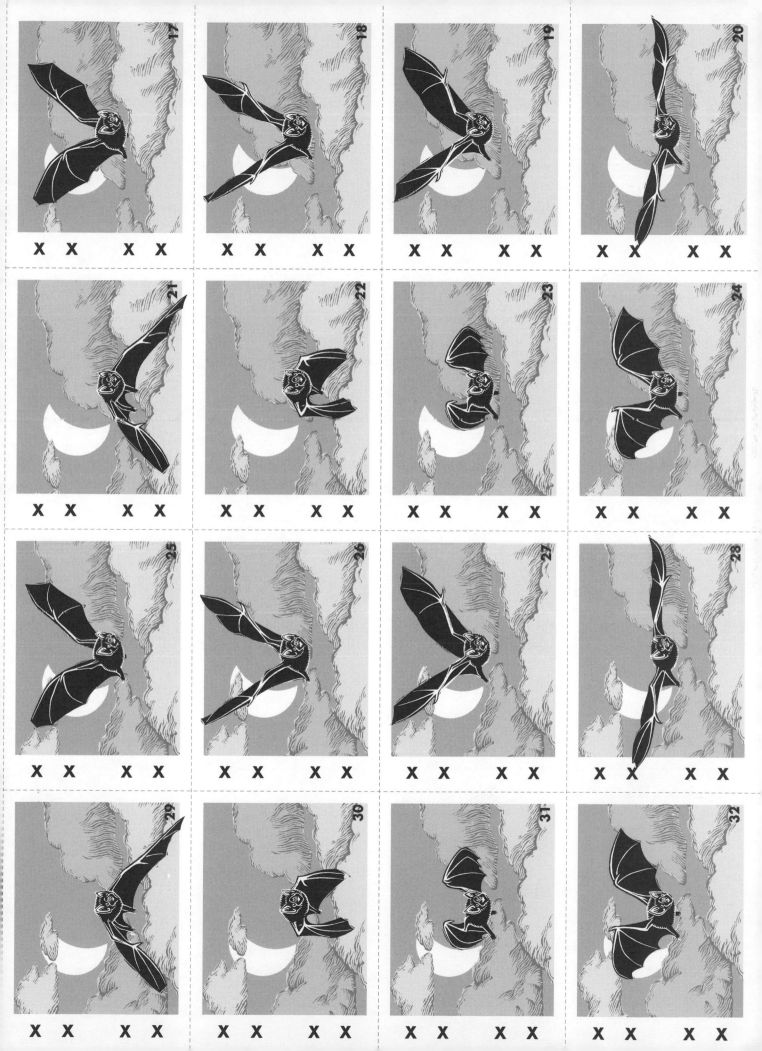

Pallid **b**ats, *Antrozous pallidus* (western North America), listen for insect footsteps and often catch their prey on the ground.

Little brown bats, *Myotis lucifugus* (North America), can ea**t** up to 600 or more insects in an hour. One every 6 seconds! Wow!

B**a**ts drink on the wing by skimming the surface of ponds and lakes.

Big brown bats, *Eptesicus fuscus* (southern Canada to extreme north of South America and West Indies), may roost and raise their you**n**g in the attics of buildings.

Bat **guano** (droppings) is mined for sale as fertilizer.

Many bats communicate with each other using sounds that humans can hear. We hear them as shrieks, chattering, and squabbling. We don't know what they mean to listening bats.

At the buggiest time of year, some bats catch all the insects they need in two half-hour hunting **s**prees a night, and take a break in between.

To cons**e**rve heat, Townsend's big-eared bats, *Plecotus townsendii* (western North America), sometimes roll up their ears and tuck them under their wings while they sleep.

Tent bats, *Uroderma bilobatum* (Central and South America), cl**i**p leaves to make a shelter.

Bats that eat large, brittle insects clip off the head, legs, and hard wing covers and eat the soft parts only. Piles of insect parts are sometimes found beneath bat roosts.

Vampire bats walk, jump, hop, and spring on their hind legs with great agility. Most bats ca**n**not walk upright. Their hind legs are not designed for it.

Male Chapin's free-tailed bats, *Tadarida chapini* (Africa), have punk pom-pom cres**t**s of fur on their heads to attract their mates.

Bats turn r**i**ght way up to **urinate** (get rid of liquid body waste) so they don't soil themselves.

The smallest bat, Kitti's hog-nosed bat, *Craseonycteris thonglongyai* (Thailand), is the size of a **b**umblebee.

The large flying fox bat, *Pteropus vampyrus* (Java), is the largest bat, with a wingspan of up to 6 feet (1.8 m)—eagle-sized.

Twenty Questions

___ 1. Some bats are as small as bumblebees. ☐

___ 2. Bats do not drink; they get enough moisture from food. ☐

___ 3. Little brown bats catch about five insects an hour. ☐

___ 4. To get enough food, bats have to hunt all night without stopping. ☐

___ 5. Some bats have such good ears, they can hear insect footsteps. ☐

___ 6. Bats are blind. ☐

___ 7. Some bats cut leaves to make tents in which to live. ☐

___ 8. All bats run fast on their long, strong legs. ☐

___ 9. Some male bats honk loudly to attract their mates. ☐

___ 10. Bats in Antarctica are white to blend with the snow. ☐

___ 11. Baby bats hatch from eggs the size of marbles. ☐

___ 12. Bats build nests in caves for their large families. ☐

___ 13. Some bats sleep with their eyes covered by their face skin. ☐

___ 14. In crowded caves, mother bats find their pups by smell and voice. ☐

___ 15. Big brown bats may roost and raise pups in attics of buildings. ☐

___ 16. Some bats roll their ears up to conserve heat. ☐

___ 17. Some bats are known to live thirty years, or more, in the wild. ☐

___ 18. Bats even **urinate** (get rid of liquid waste) upside down. ☐

___ 19. Some bats in Africa have fancy tufts of fur on their heads. ☐

___ 20. The feathers on a bat's wings help keep them warm. ☐

BAT-O-GRAM

_ _ _ _   _ _ _ _ _   _ _ _   _ _ _ _ _ _ _

The Legend of the Vampire

Have you heard of the dreaded Count Dracula? He lives in a gothic castle in Transylvania. He wears a long, black cloak over his elegant evening clothes. Notice his sharp, pointed teeth? At night he rises, in the form of a bat, and goes out to suck blood from his victims. From sunrise to sunset he sleeps in a coffin. Yes, he is the vampire of stories, movies, and comic books. He is pure fiction!

Long before the writer, Bram Stoker, wrote the story of Dracula in 1897, people in many parts of eastern Europe believed other vampire legends. These legends told that vampires, spirits of the "undead," returned from the grave to haunt the living. If a man died unexpectedly, people thought a vampire had killed him. There was no truth to these legends. They came from people's ignorance about the spread of illnesses.

When Columbus and other early explorers came to Central America, they saw for the first time real bats that drank blood. They sent word of the discovery back to Europe. Can you guess what people named the new bats? Vampires! The legend gave the name to the real creature and not the reverse.

Vampire Bats

Dracula has given vampires a bad reputation. What is the truth about vampire bats?

To set the record straight:

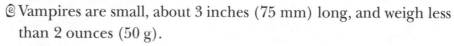

- Vampires are small, about 3 inches (75 mm) long, and weigh less than 2 ounces (50 g).
- Vampires do not drink pints of blood, nor do they suck blood.
- Vampires do not live in the United States.
- Vampires are "nice guys" to others of their kind. They adopt orphans and risk their own lives to help other vampires in need.

Only three species of bats are true vampires that drink blood. The only common one is the common vampire, *Desmodus rotundus*, that lives in Latin America. It feeds mainly on easy-to-find cattle, horses, and other domestic animals. It rarely feeds on people. Like all bats, it feeds at night. It flies to within a few yards of its prey, then walks the rest of the way. (Yes, it is agile on the ground.) It climbs onto the prey and makes a tiny shallow cut with its razor-sharp upper canine and incisor teeth. It laps the flowing blood with its tongue. Its saliva contains a special **anticoagulant**—a substance that stops blood clots forming. It usually eats one or two tablespoonfuls of blood.

Like all other mammals, some bats, vampires included, become infected with rabies. People used to think bats carried rabies without getting sick. This is not true. Bats are no different from other mammals, such as foxes and raccoons, that get this disease. They soon become sick and die. People can get rabies from a bat bite, but it's not likely to happen if you don't try to handle bats. First, bats don't go around biting people for the fun of it. Bats rarely bite, except in self-defense if they are handled. Second, very few bats have rabies (less than one in two hundred).

Common sense says that it is not normal behavior if you see any kind of bat out in the open or lying on the ground. The bat may be sick. DO NOT pick it up. Leave it alone.

The Real Batman

Dr. Merlin Tuttle has done so much to change people's opinions in favor of bats that he might almost be called the real batman.

"I was always interested in nature," Dr. Tuttle explained in an interview. "When I began my studies, there was so much to discover and so little known about bats, I simply couldn't resist satisfying my curiosity."

Dr. Tuttle's fascination with bats, which began before he finished high school, led him to become an internationally recognized bat researcher, bat photographer, author, educator, and conservation leader. Lucky for bats he chose to study them!

In 1978 Dr. Tuttle was asked to write a chapter on bats for a National Geographic Society book. When he saw the photographs that would illustrate his writing, he was horrified. The bats looked ferocious, snarling in self-defense.

"By the time these photos were enlarged for publication, their tiny teeth could have passed for those of saber-toothed tigers," Dr. Tuttle said, in an article in *Bats*, the publication of Bat Conservation International. It was these photos that convinced Dr. Tuttle to try photographing bats so that they looked more appealing—the way they usually look. Dr. Tuttle has photographed hundreds of species of bats all around the world. His amazing photographs show the bats hunting, grooming their babies, roosting, sipping nectar from blossoms, or flying off with fruit. The pictures have convinced many people that bats are attractive, after all.

"I like to take pictures of bats in the wild, but I also work with bats in temporary captivity," Dr. Tuttle said. "Keeping captive bats is not something anyone should try for themselves without a great deal of knowledge about bat needs," he added quickly. "It takes skill, patience, and extensive experience to work with bats." Dr. Tuttle makes a special "clucking" sound to alert the captive bats. Soon, when he "clucks," the bats will come to food in his hand.

"Bats vary in IQ and aptitude, just like people," Dr. Tuttle said. "Some learn faster than others. They learn new skills in the wild all the time." He remembers one frog-eating bat that always preferred to steal a frog that another bat had caught, rather than catch its own food.

Does Dr. Tuttle have a favorite bat?

"No, I don't have any real favorites. I've enjoyed getting to know individuals of many species. I especially like flying foxes. Frog-eating bats are bright little guys. I'm very fond of all the carnivores. I like *Centurio* (the wrinkle-faced bat)—in fact you could have heard me whooping and hollering along the trail when I last caught one."

"Some bats are actually affectionate," Dr. Tuttle added. He related a story of volunteers who raise orphaned baby flying foxes in Australia. Some bats are so faithful to their rehabilitators that they return to visit them even years after returning to the wild, sometimes bringing their pups along to meet the humans!

In 1982 Dr. Tuttle turned his talents in another direction. He was alarmed by the decline in bat numbers. He was horrified to meet many people around the world who boasted of killing bats. He decided people's attitudes must be changed. So he founded Bat Conservation International (BCI).

"Human intolerance about bats is a major cause of their decline. BCI works to change traditionally bad attitudes. Ten years ago, most people who called us wanted to know how to get rid of bats. Now, most people ask how they can attract them," Dr. Tuttle said. "An animal's cuteness is never a measure of its value. A true conservationist appreciates the whole world of nature with all its checks and balances, not just little parts of it." Dr. Tuttle thinks we should work to save "endangered systems of life," not just endangered species.

With his friendly bat photographs and his worldwide conservation organization dedicated to bat welfare, Dr. Tuttle has convinced many people that bats and their natural habitats must be allowed to flourish.

Come Home to Roost

People cannot do many things to help bats, except learn about them and speak up for them when necessary. (Would that be called going to bat for bats?) However, here is one practical suggestion to help bats.

Bats have a shortage of housing. Humans are just too tidy. We cut down dead trees. We demolish old buildings and replace them with new, bat-proof ones. Old bridges are replaced with new bridges often made from bat-unfriendly designs. We even seal off caves and mines for human safety reasons, and as a result harm bats that roost in them. The invention of excluder gates, however, is helping solve this problem. These gates keep people out of caves and mines, but allow bats to come and go freely. The gates do not change air-flow and temperature patterns, keeping the caves and mines suitable for bats.

You can help overcome the bat housing shortage by building a bat box. The plans for a simple box are given on page 57. If you enjoy more complex projects, write to Bat Conservation International, P.O. Box 162603, Austin, Texas 78716, for plans for larger bat boxes that have a high rate of success in attracting bats. Ask for a copy of their bat box plan and find out about joining their bat box research project.

Place your bat box so it faces east or southeast. It should be between 10 and 25 feet off the ground, and have a clear drop from the underneath opening.

Which bats might take up residence? Big brown bats, little brown bats, Mexican free-tailed bats, pallid bats, southeastern myotis, and Yuma myotis are the species most likely to occupy bat houses. Check a local field guide to see which species occur where you live.

Bats may not find your box for a while. It depends on how much bat activity there is in your neighborhood. Make your bat box a genuine research project. Although it is exciting to have a successful colony, it is equally important to learn what doesn't work. Experiment with your box location and keep watching!

ACTIVITY: *Build a Simple Bat Box*

To build a simple bat house buy untreated redwood or cedar boards, rough cut on one side. The rough cut side of the boards will be the inside of the bat house. The rough wood surface is easier for the bats to hang on to while roosting or moving around. "Treated" or "pressure treated" wood contains chemicals harmful to bats and should not be used. The redwood or cedar will weather well without paint or sealant which may also contain harmful chemicals.

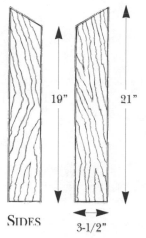

SIDES

19" 21"

3-1/2"

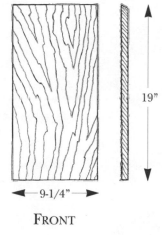

FRONT

19"

9-1/4"

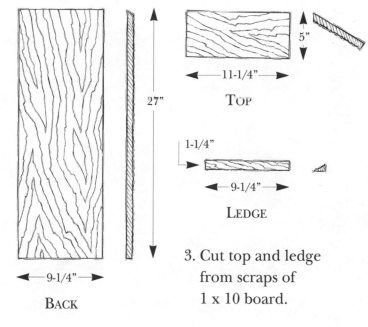

BACK

27"

9-1/4"

TOP

5"

11-1/4"

LEDGE

1-1/4"

9-1/4"

1. Cut two sides from a five foot length of 1 x 4 board. (Actual size 3/4" x 3-1/2" x 5').

2. Cut front and back from a six foot length of 1 x 10 board. (Actual size 3/4" x 9-1/4" x 6').

3. Cut top and ledge from scraps of 1 x 10 board.

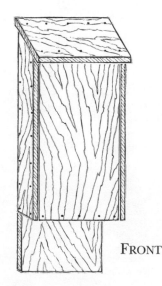

FRONT

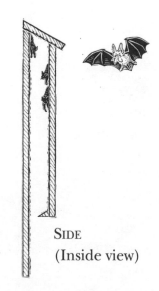

SIDE
(Inside view)

4. Use 4-penny galvanized nails to attach the ledge to the inside front.

5. Use 6-penny galvanized nails to attach sides to front and back.

6. Place roof so it is flush with back, and overhangs sides and front by about one inch. Use 6-penny galvanized nails to attach roof to sides, front, and back.

7. Use silicon caulk (which will not harm the bats) to seal all joints from the outside. This will keep the roosting bats warm and dry.

Beauty and the Beast

Suppose you were asked to judge a beauty contest among the six animals shown on this page. How would you rate them for appeal and cuteness? Use a scale of 1 to 6, 1 being the cutest.

Conduct a survey among your friends. Ask each friend to tell you which animal he or she believes to be the most beautiful. Put a check by the animal's name each time it wins a vote.

Who's the Cutest of Them All?

Koala _____

Panda _____

Bat _____

Eagle _____

Otter _____

Warthog _____

Did bats win this time? People spend more time, effort, and money trying to save animals that they find cute and appealing. But cute looks have nothing to do with how important animals are in the whole web of life. Many people still do not think of bats as appealing, but bats still need our help.

Bats are in peril for many reasons.

- Bat habitat, from tropical rainforest to temperate riverbanks and wetlands, continues to be destroyed.
- Pesticides have changed the balance of insect life, killing good and bad insects alike. Bats no longer have a reliable supply of insects in much of their former habitat. Even if pest insects become resistant to chemicals and their populations build again, it's too late. The bats are gone.
- When the bats are gone, the remaining insects flourish, causing worse damage than before. People use stronger pesticides instead of relying on bats—nature's own pest-controllers.
- Bats that catch insects heavily laden with chemicals may become ill or die.
- Misunderstanding and fear of bats have led to mass killings and the destruction of bat roosts.
- Bats are harvested for food by some people.

Bat populations are declining all over the world. These clean, gentle animals are at risk not because of any harm they do, but because of the harm people do to them. In times past, we did not realize the important part bats played in the whole web of life. Now we are beginning to learn.

Without bats . . .

- Hundreds of kinds of plants could cease to produce fruit and might eventually die out.
- Clear-cut patches of tropical forest might never grow again to their former richness and beauty.
- The world would lose miraculous pesticide-free insect control.
- We could no longer marvel at the perfect design and fascinating lives of these captivating mammals.

Without us . . .

@ Bats would be spared the effects of our toxic chemicals.
@ Bats would be spared the loss of their habitat.
@ Bats would be spared willful destruction from hate and ignorance.
@ Bats would be spared careless disturbance of their roosts in caves.

Humans are the problem, but we can also be the solution! We can work to save habitat all over the world. We can learn to use fewer pesticides. We can become bat-wise and stop the killing of bats because of ignorance and hate. Challenge your family and friends with "Bat Twenty Questions." See if they are bat-wise. Help spread the word! And as bat-wisdom increases, the world will be a better place for bats and humans alike.

60

Glossary

anticoagulant (AHN-tee-koh-ag-yuh-luhnt)— a substance that prevents blood from clotting

calcar (KAL-kahr)— a bony ankle spur that helps support a bat tail membrane

defecate (DEF-ih-kayt)— pass solid waste (droppings) from the body

diversity (duh-VUHR-suht-ee)— many different species living in the same area

echolocation (ehk-oh-loh-KAY-shun)— the use of reflected sound (echoes) to locate objects

endangered (ihn-DAYN-juhrd)— at risk of becoming extinct

glean (GLEEN)— collect bit by bit

guano (GWAHN-oh)— bat droppings

habitat (HAB-uh-tat)— the natural home of an animal

hibernate (HEYE-buhr-nayt)— spend the winter in an inactive state

homeothermic (hoh-mee-uh-THUHR-mik)— able to generate heat to maintain a constant body temperature

insectivore (in-SEK-tuh-VOHR)— an animal that feeds on insects

interfemoral membrane (in-TUHR-fem-OHR-uhl MEM-brayn)— a piece of skin that stretches between a bat's hind legs and tail

keystone species (KEE-stohn SPEE-sheez)— species whose loss would cause many other plants and animals to die out

larynx (LAR-ihngks)— part of the body that produces sound, sometimes called a voice box

lek (LEHK)— a courting ground where some animal species gather to find mates

mammary glands (MAM-uh-ree glandz)— glands of female mammals that produce milk

migrate (MEYE-grayt)— travel seasonally from one place to another and back

nectar (NEK-tuhr)— sweet liquid made by plants to attract pollinating bats, birds, or insects

nocturnal (NHAHK-tuhrn-uhl)— active at night

nose leaves (NOHZ LEEVZ)— fleshy, stand-up flaps of skin on the nose

order (AWRD-uhr)— a category of living things

predator (PRED-uht-uhr)— an animal that kills other animals for food

prey (PRAY)— an animal hunted and eaten by another animal

primate (PREYE-mayt)— the highest order of mammals, including monkeys, apes, and humans

pulses (PUHLS-uhs)— quick patterns of sound that bats emit in echolocation

pup (PUHP)— a baby bat

riparian (ruh-PEHR-ee-uhn)— along the banks of a river

roost (ROOST) — a place where bats rear young, hibernate, or temporarily rest; also—as a verb—to rest in such a place

species (SPEE-sheez)— group of animals that are alike and can interbreed

stalactite (stuh-LAK-teyet)— a formation that hangs from the ceiling of a cave

torpor (TAWR-puhr)— a state of lowered body activity which can conserve energy

tragus (TRAY-guhs)— structure in the ears of some bats that helps echolocation

ultrasonic (UHL-truh-SAHN-ihk)— sounds of very high pitch

urinate (YUHR-uh-nayt)— get rid of liquid body waste (urine)

Bibliography

Bat Conservation International. 1991. *Educator's Activity Book About Bats.* Bat Conservation International, Austin, Texas.

Fenton, M. Brock. 1992. *Bats.* Facts on File, Inc., New York, New York, and Oxford, United Kingdom.

* Halton, Cheryl Mays. 1991. *Those Amazing Bats.* Dillon Press, Inc., New York, New York.

Hill, J.H. and J.D. Smith. 1984. *Bats: A Natural History.* University of Texas Press, Austin, Texas.

* Hopf, Alice. 1985. *Bats.* Dodd Mead and Company, New York, New York.

* Jarrell, Randall. 1963. *The Bat Poet.* Macmillan Company, New York, New York.

* Johnson, Sylvia A. 1985. *The World of Bats.* Lerner Publications Co., Minneapolis, Minnesota.

* Lovett, Sarah. 1991. *Extremely Weird Bats.* John Muir Publications, Santa Fe, New Mexico.

* Pringle, Laurence. 1982. *Vampire Bats.* William Morrow and Company, New York, New York.

* Pringle, Laurence and M.D. Tuttle. 1991. *Batman: Exploring the World of Bats.* Charles Scribner's Sons, New York, New York.

Tuttle, M.D. 1988. *America's Neighborhood Bats.* University of Texas Press, Austin, Texas.

* Zoobooks. 1989. *Bats.* Wildlife Education, Ltd. (Frye and Smith, San Diego, California).

Video: Survival Anglia. 1992. *The Secret World of Bats.* BCI, Austin, Texas.

Suitable for young readers.

Seeing Bats

Look for bats on warm, still summer nights:

@ near ponds and lakes, or along streams, rivers, or canals.

@ in leafy parks and gardens, especially those with water nearby.

@ around lights at ballparks and outdoor arenas. Bats are not drawn to lights, but to the insects that the lights attract.

See large bat flights (best in July–August) at:

@ Carlsbad Caverns National Park, New Mexico (Mexican free-tailed bats)

@ Congress Avenue Bridge, Austin, Texas (Mexican free-tailed bats)

@ Blowing Wind Cave, Decatur, Alabama (endangered gray bats)

@ Point Reyes National Seashore, California (Yuma myotis)

@ Nickajack Cave, Chattanooga, Tennessee (gray bats)

See two or more species of bats up close at the following zoos*:

@ Audubon Park and Zoological Garden, New Orleans, Louisiana

@ Biodome of Montreal, Quebec, Canada

@ Busch Gardens, Tampa, Florida

@ Calgary Zoo, Alberta, Canada

@ Central Park Zoo, New York, New York

@ Chicago Zoological Park (Brookfield), Brookfield, Illinois

@ Cincinnati Zoo and Botanical Garden, Cincinnati, Ohio

@ Denver Zoo, Denver, Colorado

@ Fort Worth Zoological Park, Fort Worth, Texas

@ Houston Zoological Gardens, Houston, Texas

@ Jacksonville Zoological Park, Jacksonville, Florida

@ Los Angeles Zoo, Los Angeles, California

@ Metro Washington Park Zoo, Portland, Oregon

@ Metropolitan Toronto Zoo, Toronto, Ontario, Canada

@ Milwaukee County Zoo, Milwaukee, Wisconsin

@ Minnesota Zoological Garden, Apple Valley, Minnesota

@ National Zoological Park, Washington, D.C.

@ New York Zoological Park, New York, New York

@ Omaha's Henry Doorly Zoo, Omaha, Nebraska

@ Philadelphia Zoological Garden, Philadelphia, Pennsylvania

@ The Phoenix Zoo, Phoenix, Arizona

@ Point Defiance Zoo and Aquarium, Tacoma, Washington

@ Gladys Porter Zoo, Brownsville, Texas

@ Sedgewick County Zoo and Botanical Gardens, Wichita, Kansas

@ St. Louis Zoological Park, St. Louis, Missouri

@ Staten Island Zoo, New York, New York

@ Ellen Trout Zoo, Lufkin, Texas

@ Henry Vilas Zoo, Madison, Wisconsin

@ Woodland Park Zoo, Seattle, Washington

Zoo collections change—even if your local zoo is not listed, ask them if they have bats.

Answer Key

HANGING OUT WITH BATS,
pages 16 and 17

 Townsend's Big-eared Bat

 American False Vampire

 Straw-colored Fruit Bat

 Greater Horseshoe Bat

 Spotted Bat

 Fishing Bat

 Frog-eating Bat

 Pallid Bat

TWENTY QUESTIONS, page 51

T	1.	B	F	11.	I
F	2.	A	F	12.	G
F	3.	T	T	13.	B
F	4.	S	T	14.	E
T	5.	B	T	15.	N
F	6.	R	T	16.	E
T	7.	I	T	17.	F
F	8.	N	F	18.	I
T	9.	G	T	19.	T
F	10.	B	F	20.	S

BAT-O-GRAM, page 51
Bats bring big benefits

Acknowledgments

The Denver Museum of Natural History appreciates the encouragement, time, and support of the following individuals and organizations:

Project Sponsors—Valerie Gates and the Colorado Division of Wildlife

Publication Coordinator—Betsy R. Armstrong

Technical Review—Rick Adams, President, Colorado Bat Society; Steven Bissell, Head of Wildlife Education, Colorado Division of Wildlife; Bob Hoff, Historian, Carlsbad Caverns National Park; Pat Jablonsky, Director, Carlsbad Museum; and Merlin D. Tuttle, Director, Bat Conservation International, Inc.

The Museum's Technical and Educational Team—Elaine Anderson, Diana Lee Crew, Joyce Herold, Dr. Cheri Jones, Karen Nein, Leslie Newell, and Peggy Zemach

Design—Gail Kohler Opsahl

Cover Illustration—Gail Kohler Opsahl

Illustration—Gail Kohler Opsahl and Marjorie C. Leggitt

Thanks to Tim Barrier's fourth grade class at Graland School, who tested the activities: Susie An, Jud Brown, Nicole Burt, Ben Curtiss-Lusher, Sarah Dougherty, Martha Douglas, Aaron Dunn, Laura Goldhamer, Allison Green, Dane Harbaugh, Emma Hayward, Nils Holum, Austin Kiessig, Rebecca Lewis, Geoff McFarlane, Jenny Prosser, Christina Reed, Natalie Tate, Megan Wagner, and Mia Wiessner.